Life: a journey and a gift

Sharon Crerar

BookLeaf Publishing

India | USA | UK

Presentation by *BookLeaf Publishing*

Web: www.bookleafpub.com

E-mail: info@bookleafpub.com

ISBN:9789358317312

First edition 2023

DEDICATION

I would like to dedicate this book to Jennifer, Kerin, Jean, Rebecca, and Jean who have always encouraged me to keep writing; I love you all.

Sometimes

Sometimes just when I think I'm on the right track,
A trigger from the past can spin me straight back,
In to the depths of hopeless despair,
And suddenly I feel as if I'm still there,
Stuck in a prison with no fences or wires,
An unwilling slave to one man's desires,
No chance to escape with no money to flee,
Freedom just one of the things taken from me,
I struggled each day to find a reason to live,
Knowing I really had no more to give,
More and more was expected as days went by,
I was never enough no matter how hard I tried.

Shine

Immersed in the tranquillity of silence,
In the moments just before dawn,
I revel in my solitude,
And feel my energy restored.

Each day we all make choices,
We can change our path at any time,
Every one of us has made mistakes,
It's a human trait we can't deny.

It's what we do day after day,
That shows who we truly are,
So live your truth and shine your light,
It is bound to take you far.

Is it worth it?

Is it worth it?

Sometimes I have to wonder,
If life is really worth all the pain,
Maybe I should just give up,
Can I stand and fight again?
One day I'm fairly happy,
And see life as such a blessing,
Next day it all turns upside down,
And everything is just depressing,
I will never give in or give up though,
No matter what my mind has to say,
I will keep striving for personal peace,
In which I can live out the rest of my days.

Just Disappear

I'm watching and waiting
Till the time is right,
And I'll fight for myself
With all my might,
I don't care who you are,
Or who you say you know,
I won't be bullied by anyone,
So off you go.
Take your nasty words
And your hateful lies,
Go right ahead and just
Disappear from my life.

Perhaps Tomorrow

My imagination searches
For a way to ease the pain,
A chance to chase away the blues
That dawn with each new day.

Dreams are no escape
From the misery I hide,
Too often dreams of violence
Play over in my mind.

The only hope I cling to
That gets me through each day,
Is that, perhaps tomorrow
Some good will come my way.

Moving on.

Beneath your calm exterior,
Raging violence lurks inside,
And when you're under pressure,
It becomes too hard to hide.
Your self-control starts crumbling,
Frighteningly clear for all to see,
I will no longer take your excuses,
Or any more anger directed at me.
For years I tried to ignore it,
But it's become too much to bear,
You tell me that you love me,
You think this proves you care.
But violence is never the answer,
It will no longer make me stay,
I can finally see the truth,
And that's why I'm leaving today.

Bright Future

Hair as fine as new spun silk,
Skin as pure as farm fresh milk,
Hearts free from pains yet to come,
Enveloped in a mother's love,
Ten little fingers and matching toes,
And the very cutest tiny nose,
A smile to melt the coldest heart,
In our lives a cherished part,
Their love a prize we should enjoy
And fight whoever would destroy,
Children are our future's light,
So love them well and keep them bright.

My Repose

At ease I rest upon the dock
And calmly gaze in to the sea,
The only way I can escape
The confines that are me.

Beside the tranquil water
I watch the fish glide by,
I can feel myself relaxing,
Relief so strong I sigh.

The sun that gently warms my face
Seems to seep right through my skin,
I slip in to a calmer state
And find myself within.

The sounds of nature

How sweet the sounds of birds at play,
That lures me from my room,
Inviting me from solitude,
They chase away the gloom.

Their morning song can lift my heart,
To heights so far I sigh,
Released my mind can soar away,
And I feel like I could fly.

Each morning now as I awake,
Their beauty lights my day,
Their joyful cries mark nights end,
How sweet their sounds of play.

Appearances can deceive

I see you leaning casually against the wall,
Relaxed with easy arms and bended knee,
Eyes open and quick with life,
Clothed in your suit of security,
Marked clearly with the appropriate labels,
But I believe things are not as they seem,
Your smile appears almost too wide,
And your breathing is shallow and quick,
Beads of perspiration have formed on your
brow,
Marking your nervousness for the astute to see,
Your outward guise belies your inner turmoil,
We are not so different you and me.

Show me

Show me who you are
Not your lifestyle
Or your car
They are not important
Speak only your truth
Not repetition of another's
Ghastly regurgitation
Meant to impress
Show me who you are
You
You are not a job
You are so much more
Show me who you are
Without words
Show me the truth at your core
Show me more.

Anxiety and me

What does anxiety do to you?
Does it leave you frozen with fear in a room?
Are you too scared to walk out the front door?
All based on traumas inflicted before,
Do you shake from your head down to your
feet?
Do you stammer or find it hard to speak?
Do you feel physically sick when angry voices
are raised?
To the point of being in bed for days,
I'm still triggered when I go in to a bank
30 years has yet to make a change to that,
I've done decades of intense counselling too,
And finally I realised the absolute truth,
Past traumas are imprinted on my soul,
But I will never let them make me less whole,
So I'll fight anxiety as long as I need,
Until the day
I'm finally
Free

Peace to me

Slowly but surely as each day unfolds,
I'm learning more of what heals my soul,
Laughter, love, time with good friends,
Eases a load that never seems to end,

A trip to the beach to soak up some sun,
Making a sand angel is my sort of fun,
Crystal clear water calls loudly to me,
"Throw yourself in and feel the love of the sea"

Time in the garden and feet in the dirt,
Makes me appreciate our beautiful earth,
A walk through the bush marvelling at all I can
see
These are the things that bring true peace to me.

Consumptive Curse

There's a world outside my window,
If I could only dare to look,
It's safer for me to hide away,
To lose myself within a book,
Where people care for others,
With war a forgotten fear,
Where animals can speak,
Knowing human beings can hear,
Where our planet is our biggest jewel,
Why can't we acknowledge its true worth?
Before the entire world is torn apart,
By modern man's consumptive curse.

Tarnished Knight

I thought you were my knight,
Come to save the day,
To rescue me from poverty,
Shame on me for thinking that way,
I thought my reward for hardships suffered,
Had been sent to me as you,
My punishment for thinking that,
Was nine years of relentless abuse,
I thought I had deserved it,
For trying to take the easy path,
It certainly didn't turn out like that,
But you fooled me from the start,
Your sister told you all there was,
To know about my life,
You took it in and twisted things,
Till control was no longer mine,
You pretended to be a caring person,
But that was all a farce,
I loved the face you showed in public,
But not the truth behind the mask,
By the time you showed me the real you,
It was just too late,
I'd given up my home and freedom,
To be treated as your slave.

Pretender

Scratch the thin veneer of your calm exterior,
You can see the raging violence that lurks inside,
And it's when you're under pressure,
That the truth becomes too hard to hide,
The charade you've built starts crumbling,
It's a frightening thing to actually see,
But I will no longer make excuses
For any more anger directed at me,
For too long I've protected your image,
I told myself it was my cross to bear,
You kept telling me you loved me,
How does hurting me prove you care?
Violence is never a solution,
Fear will no longer make me stay,
I've taken too many of your lessons,
I will no longer be part of your public display.

My search

Tranquillity I have sought you
In so many different ways,
From meditation with the rising sun,
To diving under the bluest silky waves,
Serenity you have eluded me,
So far along life's path,
I'm determined to keep searching,
Every day is a fresh new start.
Peace you have seemed so distant,
Kept at bay by tormented dreams,
I will always strive to reach you,
No matter how far away you seem,
Happiness you always seemed to me,
Something everybody else could find,
Now I know you have many faces,
And I've seen glimpses of you all my life,
Love you are an enigma,
Sometimes flimsy other times solid as a rock,
Though I have yet to find you romantically,
My quest to understand you will never stop.

Just a rabbit

To farmers I'm just a menace,
I bring devastation to your land,
But I did not choose to emigrate,
In that I see man's hand.
In years gone by you shipped us here,
With thoughts of sport in mind,
How can you now blame me,
For making your land mine?
In groups of two or three or more,
You hunt us down at night,
Then when you're finally ready
Line us up in rifle sights,
A cry goes up your kill is made,
A hunter's pride is clear to see,
You think my tail will bring you luck?
It didn't work for me,
With one quick shot you end my life
And blow my dreams away,
Just so you can have a charm
To keep bad luck at bay.

Crumbs

Stop squabbling like children
Fighting over some sweets,
Stop posturing like bullies,
Brawling over a street,
For Australia's sake grow up,
It's way beyond time,
The people are quite simply,
Sick and tired of your lies,
Your blatant greed and misogyny
With high paid jobs for old chums,
Leaves those without your privilege
To survive on mere crumbs.

I can't

I can't block out the past as you expect me to,
I can't pretend it didn't happen like you do,
I can't wipe out the pain you inflicted on my
heart,
The future we make is linked to the past,
I know what it is to feel unwanted and alone,
Your role in my torment is something you'll
never own,
Without looking back and resolving the past,
Healing our relationship could never start,
Our family unit was all a big sham,
I'm finally realising you couldn't give a damn.

Solar Lights

Solar lights you beckon me,
With your colour changing majesty,
Red to blue to white then green,
You illuminate the night's soft scenes,
You spread your glow across the pond,
And show to whom the night belongs,
In peaceful quiet solitude,
I'm enveloped by your gentle hues,
Enjoying tranquil night time sounds,
This is where my bliss is found.